YOUR KNOWLEDGE HAS VALUE

Nicola Gundrum

Are Mutual Fund Managers better than us?

Is it beneficial to engage a mutual fund manager? Duties, liability, performance.

GRIN Verlag

Bibliografische Information der Deutschen Nationalbibliothek:

Die Deutsche Bibliothek verzeichnet diese Publikation in der Deutschen National-
bibliografie; detaillierte bibliografische Daten sind im Internet über http://dnb.d-
nb.de/ abrufbar.

Imprint:

Copyright © 2011 GRIN Verlag GmbH
Druck und Bindung: Books on Demand GmbH, Norderstedt Germany
ISBN: 978-3-656-29983-7

This book at GRIN:

http://www.grin.com/en/e-book/203397/are-mutual-fund-managers-better-than-us

GRIN - Your knowledge has value

Der GRIN Verlag publiziert seit 1998 wissenschaftliche Arbeiten von Studenten, Hochschullehrern und anderen Akademikern als eBook und gedrucktes Buch. Die Verlagswebsite www.grin.com ist die ideale Plattform zur Veröffentlichung von Hausarbeiten, Abschlussarbeiten, wissenschaftlichen Aufsätzen, Dissertationen und Fachbüchern.

Visit us on the internet:

http://www.grin.com/

http://www.facebook.com/grincom

http://www.twitter.com/grin_com

Shanghai University
Assignment

Area of expertise: Finance

Topic: Are mutual fund managers better than us?

Is it beneficial to engage a mutual fund manager? Duties, liability, performance.

Submitted by: Nicola Gundrum

Submitted on: 29 April 2011

Are Mutual Fund Managers Better Than Us?

What is a fund manager?

Many people want to invest their money with the aim to gain a profit. Some let their capital administrate by mutual fund managers. Others try to invest their money by their own. Is it more effective to engage a professional fund manager or to do it by your own? This question will be analyzed and answered in the following paragraphs.

Fund manager are professional acting property administrators that manage the capital of the investors especially in money market funds, pension funds, mutual stock funds, real estate investment funds, balanced funds and fund of hedge funds. Moreover they should be able to augment the money of the investors above the average addition. In most cases they are measured by benchmarks. They administrate the investment asset pool by trying to invest the assets as ratably as possible. During this process they consider the chances of their own taken risks. Furthermore they do the exact decisions referring the capital assets in which a fund invests. It depends on the fund manager if the fund satisfied its investors with a good performance or if just a small performance is reached.[1]

According to German law it can be said that there is a trinomial structure in case of mutual funds. The licensed asset management company collects money from the investors in one or more funds and administrates it with the aim to make a profit. The capital of the funds is separately from the capital of the fund manager stored as special property at the depositary bank and it is administrated according to the fund manager's instructions. Issuance and return of the fund shares are carried out through the depositary bank. A fund must have contract conditions which indicate aim, purpose, investment strategy, accountability rules and charge fee of the administrator.[2]

---

[1] **Stobitzer, C.** (2009).
[2] **Mieland, M.** (2006).

Duties

Duties are important referring to the investors. They support their aims and wishes. Furthermore they delimit selfish acting of mutual fund managers. Therefore the duties might help to reach a high performance and minimize risks. They are important to establish trust between investors and mutual fund managers.

Referring to decisions with the offered duty to take care, the fund manager has not only to consider the changes of the stock, but also he has to know about the investment conditions and the investment policy of the fund as well as about the regulations by law.

Liabilities, which violation leads to claims for damages, can be regulated by law or by the memorandum of association. They can be exactly formulated and instructed, but also they can be circumscribed in more or less opened valuations terms. The duty catalogues determine what a fund manager in details is allowed to do, have to do and what should be neglected.

Therefore some important duties are:

Duty to take care:

The general main liability is the duty to administrate the investment fund with the diligence of a prudent businessman; with solely interest of the investors and the aim of performance or to earn reliable profits. According to this process the fund manager must have an extremely wide scope for judgment evaluation (Business Judgment Rule)[3], as far as the reliability to a careful course of action it not due to the precise decision basis, the interest of the investors to maintain the profitability or referring to certain situations like the danger to go bankrupt.

Courts are not allowed to put their own judgment in lieu of the commercial opinion of the fund manager, even though if subsequently exposes that a commercial rational and fungible decision has a negative impact. Risks are unavoidable; not to take risks, but avoiding them can be blamed under certain conditions. Therefore the damage of the funds is not important, because funds always bear for the investment risk. Moreover it is determining that the

---

[3] **Strupler, C.** (2010).

disregarding of the required carefulness in the process of preparation and control of the decisions or during the monitoring of the investments because false investments cannot be avoided, but can be reduced in their frequency and damage potential through carefulness and control.

Risk minimization duty:

The protection of the investors' interest serves particularly the prohibition of the short sale as well as the regulations of the investment to avoid to big risks. For example in Germany it is only allowed that for all administrated funds a maximum of 10% of the total number of shares from one issuer can be purchased, so that a domination of the companies through funds can be avoided.[4]

Information duty:

The regulation of the right and full information of the investor requires before the selling of the shares the free availability of a purchase prospect with contract conditions for the investor. Also the publishing of yearly and half-yearly results are required as well as the daily publishing of the share prices. The fees and cost have also to be published.

Liability

Liabilities are also important to support the trust-feeling of investors referring to fund managers. All in all they have similar functions as the duties.

For the damage through the duty violation of the fund vouches the contrary to duty and culpable doers. The liability for the damage always conditions a damage of the duty. The fund manager vouches not only for failure neither referring German law nor according to foreign laws.[5]

The elements of a crime of a duty violation are indicated through a vouching of the fund manager; it means a damage of the inner carefulness is added. There is no liability easement

---

[4] **Strupler, C.** (2010).
[5] **Strupler, C.** (2010).

valid for the vouching of fund managers; therefore they are responsible for negligence and deliberate intention.[6]

Liability according to shareholder

Every investor can expect from the fund manager lawful management. The depository bank is responsible to make possible claim for damages valid. In case of failure to act a direct claim of the shareholder against the fund manager or the depository bank is possible.

Moreover the fund manager vouches if the investor had bought shares on the basis of a prospect with mistakes.

Liability referring to the state

The fund manager as a special credit institution stands under state control and has to make regularly reports. The state is able to forbid the business for a certain period of time or forever; or he can declare a monetary fine in case of violation of duty.

Insurance

Nothing is opposed to the insurance for the liability and the bonus payment for that trough the enterprises. Different insurance providers have developed a policy outline of a fund manager insurance although the insufficient claim of the depository bank against the fund manager is not insured; moreover the coverage for the deliberate intention is missing.

The recent insurance denseness is very small.[7] This implies that there is a high risk for investors in case of damages, when the fund manager does not fulfill his duties.

Of course an abstinence of such an insurance should not have a unfavorable influence on the shareholders according to the investment law. The capital assets of the funds are kept safe at the depository bank and are protected against fraud through the fund manager. If the fund manager provokes damage through a mistake, it is not allowed to pay the damage with the fund capital. An insurance would only protect the investment company itself or its

---

[6] **Strupler, C.** (2010).
[7] **Kolbinger, A.** (2011).

owners (the bank or the insurance) referring to the damage which would be regulated account of the joint capital of the company.[8]

Benchmark

Benchmark or Benchmarking terms a comparing analysis with a determined reference value. The success of a certain share is compared with the market development. In most cases an index is used as a benchmark. Referring to investment banking every fund is compared with a benchmark. This can be for example a share index. The success with German shares is measured through the DAX

The success of a share fund is measured by analyzing if it beats its benchmark or not. It makes only sense to compare a fund with a benchmark if the benchmark represents the investment universe of the fund. When the investor performs better than the DAX, then his share was successful.

The basic aim of the benchmarking is to identify weaknesses of a company and its processes through comparison with other enterprises as well as processes and to increase the performance. Either a minimum of two succeeded data acquisitions have to be performed o rat least two different objects have to be collected at the same time.[9]

Performance (risk management)

Performance is a measurement for the aim achievement. It describes the surplus of the achieved return on assets about a comparable, adequate return on benchmark. The rate of return difference is standardized through the division of an adequate degree of risk.[10]

Attribution analysis

The performance a portfolio management can be measured by an attribution analysis. The achievement can be divided into three parts:

- market-induced: passive achievement which can be understand through the progress of a benchmark

---

[8] **Kolbinger, A.** (2011).
[9] **Schlien, A.** (2011).
[10] **Hartmann-Wendels, T.** (2004).

- structural: decision according to the exchange rate fluctuation or the performance progress of different markets
- technical: trough over or under weighting of single shares[11]

Performance measurement

The measurement of the performance should not only be reduced to the evaluation of fund returns, but must also include other fund parts which are in the interest of the investors (like the measure of risk taken). Other elements of the performance measurement: evaluation when fund managers succeeded in achieving their objective; how they compare to their peers; as well as whether the results of the portfolio management were due to luck or the skills of the manager.[12]

At this point it is very important to mention that there is a modern portfolio theory which established the quantitative link that connects the portfolio risk and the return. One of the first performance measurements is the Sharpe ratio. It measures the return of the portfolio in excess of the risk-free rate, compared to the total portfolio risk. This measure does not relate to any benchmark and avoids drawbacks referring to a poor choice of benchmark. The separation of the performance of the market in that the portfolio is invested from that of the manager is not allowed.[13]

The only reliable performance measure seems to be the portfolio alpha. It measures the difference between the return of the portfolio and that of a benchmark portfolio. In that case you have to distinguish between normal returns (, provided by the fair reward for portfolio exposures to different risks) and passive management (like abnormal performance because of the skills or the luck of the manager). The first element belongs to allocation and style investment choices, that probably might not be under the sole manager's control and which are depending on the economic context. The other element is an evaluation of the success achieved through the decisions of the manager. Just the latter, measured by alpha, allows the evaluation of the manager's true performance.[14]

---

[11] **Hartmann-Wendels, T.**(2004).
[12] **Hartmann-Wendels, T.** (2004).
[13] **Hartmann-Wendels, T.** (2004).
[14] **Hartmann-Wendels, T.** (2004).

The advantages and disadvantages of mutual funds

Compared to direct investing in individual securities mutual funds have several advantages:

- regulations set by the government
- diversification
- possibility of redeem daily at net asset value
- professional knowledge of the fund manager referring investment management
- ability to take part in investments that may only be available to larger investors

Disadvantages:

- fees to pay the fund manager
- less predictable income
- no chance of customizing
- less control over timing of recognition of gains and losses

Mutual fund managers and their success fees

In almost the half cases of worldwide mutual funds the success fees are paid to the fund managers. In this process it does not matter neither if the fund is in minus nor if it could reach a balancing to the earlier losses.[15]

In a lot of cases the particular success is estimated before the administration cost are discounted. This implicates double cost for the investors. Partly the aims of the investors are determined very low. The result is sometimes called to be a success if the fund is higher than zero percent.[16]

The result of doubtful acting of fund companies can signify that the investors do not profit of a higher fund return. For example the mutual stock fund Global Value has paid out to DWS in the years 2008/2009 a profit sharing of 6.7 million euro, thereby the fund return was reduced about 1,36 percent. The fund count up to one year was not better than the

---

[15] **Rohr, R.** (2010).
[16] **Rohr, R.** (2010).

particular comparing measurement. Additionally the fund looses one third of its value in one year.[17]

The basic idea of the success fees is that the fund manager should be motivated, so that he/she works harder in the interest of the investors. In many cases the result was the opposite as the fund manager were seduced to a higher readiness to assume risk. This is especially valid when the success fees are only counted up to a half year or a smaller time period – this fits to around about 20 percent of the funds. Therefore funds with a success fee earn no higher returns for the investors than funds that are not related to success fees.[18]

Mutual fund managers break seldom the index

The German share index (DAX) reached a very high level in the year 2006. A lot of investors did not make a profit because of that, but they possessed fewer shares than in the years before. Especially the banks are guilty as they recommend their costumers bad shares and not profitable mutual funds.[19]

Around 70 percent of all mutual funds come off worse than their compared stock index. For example the DAX from 2006 is three times as high as it was in the year 2002. Most funds who bought German shares did not reach such a result (like Adig Adifonds, Meag Proinvest or Activest Top Deutschland).[20]

This is not only surprisingly, but also embarrassing. High-paid and professional specialized bank manager are not able to beat the DAX. They cannot invest the capital of the investors better than every single investor could have done it by oneself – if they only had bought exactly the 30 shares which represent the DAX. Moreover the investment companies get well paid for nonperformance: Who buys a mutual stock fund has to pay an average fee of 3-5 percent.[21]

More and more investors notice this disproportion. They get their money out of the bad funds. Many funds have to give up: 228 in the year 2005. Clever investors should have a look

---

[17] **Rohr, R.** (2010).
[18] **Rohr, R.** (2010).
[19] **Dönch, U.** (2006).
[20] **Dönch, U.**(2006).
[21] **Dönch, U.** (2006).

at the recent fund ranking list and can go over to a more successful fund of the competitors.[22]

Some mutual fund managers are overpaid

The hedge fund manager John Paulson earned five billion dollar in the year 2008. This was the biggest profit of the year in the history of the branch. Half of the profit stands only on the paper because it reflects the performance of shares which can sink anytime. The other part was realized through sells. Paulson achieved four billion dollar profit with speculations of junk mortgages.[23]

The risk management becomes more and more important

Manager of the investment branch sees themselves with the question confronted how they can handle the Tail Risks, how to ensure extreme incidents like the nuclear crisis in Japan. In the future the risk management will play a more important role in the daily life of the fund managers.[24]

Some experts advice to focus more in ETFs because active funds come along with a high risk. ETFs only lose as much as the market does. There are already some fund of funds on the market which only invest in ETF.[25]

My own opinion and some additional information

I do not really trust mutual fund managers. First of all I do not think that I need someone to help me planning my financial future. While I am not certainly an expert on the subject, I feel that to set a financial plan with an "expert" is not going to be any better than purchasing a book about financial planning and doing it by myself. In that case I would save a lot of money. The managers do not have a crystal ball, so that their recommendations can still be false. If I go safe with an index fund and just invest in a lazy portfolio, will I really be that far behind? If the majority of actively managed mutual funds, staffed with the best educated and brightest working on this 24/7, can't beat the index... can an adviser?

---

[22] **Dönch, U.** (2006).
[23] **Reuters, K.** (2011).
[24] **Strupler, C.** (2010).
[25] **Strupler, C.** (2010).

Just a few fund managers are their money worth like an exclusive survey of the investment company Gecam for WELT ONLINE had analyzed. Most of the managers stick almost slavery at the particularly comparing index. There is not even a hint of an active choice of the best shares. At the end the most funds have a worse result than their comparing indexes.[26]

Gecam executive Uwe Leonhardt says that less than one percent of the fund manager leads his/her funds really active. He and his employees analyzed about 7500 funds according to their index near and also referring to their performance. They used the mathematical ratio of the coefficient of correlation for the measurement of the index orientation. A value of 1 stands for a 100% correlation to the index. This means that the fund pictures the index one to one. The smaller the value, the more free seems to be the fund manager in the composition of the fund's substance.[27]

The deflating result: 94 percent of the mutual stock funds correlate to more than 80 percent with the index. Three fourth matches about 90 percent with the index. Only one percent of this fund group has a correlation less than 0.6. Only under this value you can call it active management![28]

The results are a bit better when it comes to other fund groups. According to pension funds 21 percent can be called as active managed funds. Moreover the percentage is 41 referring to money market funds, fund of funds as well as balanced mutual funds.[29]

It seems that a lot of fund manager tried to operate against in the crisis by releasing from the index. They think they can reduce losses through a stronger independence in their investment decisions. This procedure did not work out well. Furthermore the consequence of a smaller correlation to the index is a better performance.[30]

---

[26] **Stocker, F.** (2009).
[27] **Stocker, F.** (2009).
[28] **Stocker, F.** (2009).
[29] **Stocker, F.** (2009).
[30] **Stocker, F.** (2009).

This displays the comparison of the fund groups with the best and the worst progress which were observed in a period of three years. Only one of the 25 offered energy funds could beat the benchmark.[31]

Taking all these aspects into consideration the reader might come to the conclusion that mutual fund managers are not better than us. Investing by your own is more successful, but for some reasons like lack of time and no financial knowledge, it might be better to let your capital administrate by a mutual fund manager.

(Note: Information referring laws and regulations are based on German standards because I have a higher knowledge about these facts than about other national regulations. Nevertheless other nations have similar regulations.)

---

[31] **Stocker, F.** (2009).

Bibliography

Dönch, U. (2006), Fonds-Manager sind ihr Geld nicht wert. Online document:
http://www.focus.de/finanzen/doenchkolumne/doenchs-finanz-kolumne_aid_25849.html.
(23.04.2011)

Hartmann-Wendels, T.: Bankbetriebslehre. Springer, 3. Auflage, Berlin 2004.

Kolbinger, A. (2011), Der Fondsmanager als professioneller Vermögensberater. Online documet:
http://www.wallstreet-online.de/ratgeber/finanzen-steuern-versicherung/anlagen-und-
investitionen/der-fondsmanager-als-professioneller-vermoegensverwalter. (23.04.2011)

Mieland, M.(2006), Fonds Risiken. Online document: http://www.fond.de/fonds-risiken/.
(18.04.2011)

Reuters, K. (2011), Fondsmanager verdient fünf Milliarden Dollar. Online document:
http://www.welt.de/finanzen/article12368775/Fondsmanager-verdient-fuenf-Milliarden-Dollar.html.
(14.04.2011)

Rohr, R. (2010), Investmentfonds-Manager kassieren Bonus selbst bei einem Minus der Fonds.
Online document: http://www.tarife-verzeichnis.de/nachrichten/3007-investmentfonds-manager-
kassieren-bonus-selbst-bei-einem-minus-der-fonds.html. (23.04.2011)

Schlien, A. (2011), Benchmark. Online document:
http://www.finanzentest.de/lexikon/665/Benchmark.html. (18.04.2011)

Stobitzer, C. (2009), Fondsmanager. Online document: http://www.boerse-
einsteiger.de/fondsmanager.php. (18.04.2011)

Stocker, F. (2009), Fonds-Manager sind nur Sklaven des Indexes. Online document:
http://www.welt.de/finanzen/article3465025/Fonds-Manager-sind-nur-Sklaven-der-Indizes.html.
(15.04.2011)

Strupler, C., Gasper, G. (2010), Willensvollstrecker – Rechte, Pflichten und Aufgaben. Online
document:
http://www.atgroup.ch/fileadmin/Content_Images/Broschueren/ATG_forum_ausgabe_0310_LR.pdf.
(19.04.2011)